T0199084

The Widow and Her Kids

Nora Aviles

WESTBOW
PRESS®
A DIVISION OF THOMAS NELSON
& ZONDERVAN

Scripture taken from the King James Version of the Bible.

WestBow Press books may be ordered through booksellers or by contacting:

WestBow Press
A Division of Thomas Nelson & Zondervan
1663 Liberty Drive
Bloomington, IN 47403
www.westbowpress.com
1 (866) 928-1240

ISBN: 978-1-9736-6126-9 (sc)
ISBN: 978-1-9736-6127-6 (e)

Library of Congress Control Number: 2019905114

Print information available on the last page.

WestBow Press rev. date: 05/30/2019

On many occasions, our lives are exposed by experiences that serve us to understand the feelings of those around us. There are many who, with simulated smiles, surround us by introducing themselves with an apparent control they are far from possessing.

In order to simulate the pain they feel inside, and trying on many occasions to ignore the weight that burdens their souls, they smile and play with the burdens of the day, trying to make that pain ephemeral.

I write in memory of all those who personally, or perhaps with silenced body language, showed me that pain and weariness. To refresh your memory and remind you that who cares for you is greater than the one who abandoned you.

Preface

IT IS AMAZING TO BE CONFRONTED WITH A CALL from which we know nothing or have any understanding. In my case, this astonishment was accompanied by doubts and a multitude of questions for which I could not find answers. Perhaps because of a sense of recognized insufficiency, or pure ignorance of the process, my fears produced a slow but steady pilgrimage to a sense of grateful accomplishment.

It's just self-discipline that produces in the human being a certain achievement. But when that determined achievement is produced by the unique direction of the Holy Spirit, we have only the acceptance of giving the glory to Him, who exclusively deserves it. The Lord of Lords and King of Kings, Jehovah of Armies. And in this way, we recognize the blessing obtained by serving as instruments in His hands.

Thanks

WHEN WE ARE SURPRISED BY THE CALL TO DO something we have never done, we usually resort to trying to acquire all the help that exists. However, it is not until we see the final product that we realize all things worked in harmony to be able to achieve it. Usually we do not perceive it at the moment, but by compiling the stages of the process, we understand who and when we received the help we so badly needed.

That has been the precise work of my family: my parents, my husband, and my children. I lack the words to be able to thank them for all the times that in a direct or indirect way, they taught me, pushed me, and helped me achieve what I was entrusted to do. A thousand times thanks to my kids—Suhaely, Joshua, and Will. You inspire me and have showed me a special kind of love. I am grateful that God allowed me to be called your mother. Thank you for sticking with me through thick and thin. May God repay you in every form of blessings.

I must also thank my special friends Ivette Calle, Angela Glover, Aida Burgos, and Sarah Sein. Ladies, sometimes it was a call and others a text, but I will forever appreciate how God used you even when you didn't know it. The amazing church I am part of and the unconditional help from my pastors, Joshua and Alexandra Algarin, your prayers made the difference. May God repay you.

Introduction

MANY TIMES IN LIFE WE COME ACROSS QUESTIONS for which we find no defined responses. We see so many things that are wrong and carry injustice, and our hearts fill with discouragement. We see that in all areas of life; struggles are a great part of life. And the universal question surfaces: Why does this have to happen? Females have a harder time with the issue of struggles because we are usually brought up supplied with our common needs.

But what happens in the heart of a woman who enters marriage expecting to supply the need of her husband and to be supplied as well. Then she finds her role is only to serve? Or what happens in the mind of a woman who recognizes she has a husband but is a widow in many ways. She knows he is there by her side, but the relationship is far from what she was expecting or needing. Close but yet so far.

It is there and then that many questions overtake our mind, and one must ask, "Did I make a mistake? Why is this happening, and why do I have to go through this?" I found that the process of answering this challenging question is usually what God uses to mold us into a vessel for His glory. If we look closely to the Word of God, we will find that everyone who has conquered the will of God for their lives usually came through struggle, resistance, and a great need of courage. So do not be dismayed by the struggles you are encountering. I can assure they have great purposes; they bring you closer to God and allow you to see His glory.

The Widow and Her Kids

BETWEEN THE COVERS OF THE BIBLE WE FIND stories of courageous women who endeavored to identify the work that God entrusted to them. From Genesis to Revelation, we find a diversity of calls and functions programmed by God. We notice that despite the opposition they faced, their tenacity led them to personal experiences with God. With the call, He placed trust in them, knowing that it would be completed. Some received help from those around them; others did not. But all received the grace and strength that comes from God.

One of the most important things for every human being is to feel identified with the person that God created them to be. But many, little by little, lose their identities, and deviate from the purpose for which we were created. Women have a special calling, and they run the risk of being overtaken by the daily roles they has to accomplish. Many times that call can easily be buried as a to-do chore for someday. A day that never comes.

Once Eve was presented to Adam, in Genesis 2:23, we find his initial name for her was woman. However, after she deviates from that identity and from the call God entrusted to her, in Genesis 3:20, a new name and identity are given to her. Under the name of Eve, she is the mother of all living beings. This story is one of the most disputed in the Bible. The first woman mentioned in the Bible, she carries one of the most controversial stories studied. Scholars to exegetes dispute the achievement, if any, of Eve.

In all, we notice a wide implication of guilt involved in a possible error by the One who executed the plan. The accusations include not only God but also Adam. I think one of the harshest accusations I've heard mentioned Eve as a mistake from the beginning to the end. Not only did she make Adam fall from God's grace, she also gave us the first murderer in human history, I heard another say.

For this reason, those who tend to believe—they have the right to judge—list it as one of the first failures of the human race. However, in Genesis 3:13, we note that God asks Eve, "What have you done?" Her answer is clear and definite: "The command you gave me I did not complete because the snake deceived me, and I ate" (paraphrased).

In the same way, we have to calculate that despite all its supposed failures, the serpent does not appear on the scene until Eve is created. We do not know how long Adam is alone, with the same specific instructions from God. But we do notice that Eve is created, and a new character is named in the scene, the serpent. The appearance of it brings us the clarity of understanding that to complete the call in our lives, there will always be battles we have to fight.

Eve's answer to God's question shows that she studied the plan, reviewed the faults executed, assumed responsibility, and declared her error. This is the precise restoration process. God does not work with someone who does not recognize his or her mistakes. Eve did not accuse anyone. She simply said (to paraphrase), "I did exactly what you told me not to do." Few people can be noticed to have that kind of sincerity and openness.

After the fall, we also notice in Genesis 3:15 that God Himself gives Eve a new task. That is to spread the human race so that through it would come He, who would wound the head of the serpent—Jesus Christ. The creation of Eve produced a movement in the garden of Eden from the serpent. Independently, Adam was created first. So we must ask, why did the serpent focus on Eve and not Adam? What did Eve represent that made the serpent focus on stopping her and why?

As we mentioned before, if we evaluate the scene up to here, many would probably determine that Eve's life was a complete failure. However, it is worth detailing that this is the same Eve who serves as a vehicle for the human race to gain access to the world. But her story does not end there. History rementions her and explains that her relationship with God continued despite her error. She herself pronounces in Genesis 4:25 that God replaced a son (Set) for Abel.

It seems that the one that many determine as a failure, God uses for a specific plan. God does not reward the wicked, but He does restore the fallen. Her error did not stop her; nor did the snake. Her husband's inability to guide and protect her did not stop her life from being productive in other areas. That is the preciousness of our God. No matter how great the mistake we have made, provided there is true repentance, there will be restoration.

AND THAT'S WHERE WE FIND THE FIRST CALL about women. Even though Adam was created first and called to guide, care for, and protect Eve, we independently noticed there was a task that she had to complete. Her husband could perhaps help her to a certain extent, but it was she who would spread the human race, despite his mistake. God still loved her. He would work hard, and she would reproduce whatever he provided. God gave them both a clean slate, a fresh start, a new beginning.

We live in a condemnatory generation that, instead of educating, judges. But with God, things are different. As parents, we face the need to educate our girls to understand that before receiving love and acceptance of any other person, they first must learn to love and respect themselves. Otherwise, they may go out to find a love that they do not understand or know how it works. We need to feel loved. And it is that need that sends us to look for it blindly.

This is where many face the decisive moment of remaining identified with who they were before entering marriage or succumb to the ideals of a spouse. Some have the happiness that their spouse seeks the presence of God to guide his life and that of his family. Others do not receive that guidance. They run the risk of being stuck and oblivious to what God called them to do. This is why there is a need to have a personal relationship with God before entering a mortal relationship.

It is very easy for a woman to think, *God called man to be the head of the home, so it is for my husband, not me, to figure out how this is going to work*. But we have to stop and study everything that is at stake. Let's think about that from this point of view. How important are the upbringing and education of your children? What education did you think about first, the spiritual or secular?

What are the risks our children face if they do not have the correct upbringing? Well, remember that if you are a widow, without the guidance and priesthood of your husband, your children lack a father in that sense also. It's true that our children will become adults, and they will make their own mistakes. But how will you feel if you know that you failed in their upbringing, and for that reason, they are in trouble? Even if your husband does not take the plan designed by God with due seriousness, can that be a justified reason before God to shield you from your responsibility?

Is there something you can do for yourself and your children, with or without your husband? There is a portion of a verse in Jeremiah 31:22 that says, "The Lord creates something new in the land ... A female will shelter a man." And sometimes, we have to do exactly that. It might be that he is struggling spiritually, and you will have to shield him.

IT MIGHT BE HE HAS COME TO A SPIRITUAL WALL and does not know what to do. You will have to help him overcome his confusion and sort it out. In anything and everything, remember you are designed by God to be his helper, so be who He created you to be, regardless what you think, see, and feel. Let God judge the rest.

One of the biggest problems of this generation is the created dependency that most people have. So we must be really alert and wise to discern the difference between created and naturally occurring dependency. Otherwise, we become complacent, relying on others for what we can do. This problem is noticed in all facets of the human being. It is one thing to be a helper to each other, and it is another to grow lazy and dependent.The biggest mistake that a human being can commit is not to give God His due honor; it is He who designed the perfect role for everyone.

The first thing we should do in everything that we are considering to undertake, if we want it to be successful, is place it in the hands of God for direction. The same happens with our relationships. We know stories of couples who have been married for decades. All declare that it has not been easy. Others note that their marriages do not last long. So what produces a lasting marriage? Is it love? Is it desire? Is it affinity? Approaching God in search of His direction?

Now, what happens in the heart of someone who directs one's heart to God, and after joining with that other person, realizes the other's service to God lost its strength. Being a woman, I have to speak from a woman's point of view. What happens in the heart of a woman who gets married for all the right reasons but ends up disappointed and discouraged? Or to the one who marries her prince, and after a while, he turns into a frog, whose actions no longer reveal that he has been with God? What does a woman do who notices that her children have become orphans of the bond a child and father should have, which directs and shapes the character of children?

How does that woman feel when she feels weak in faith and does not see her husband notice it and cover her with his prayer and intercession? Or maybe guides her to the Word of God. Remember, we are detailing the disappointment that we feel spiritually speaking; talking about everyday disappointment would not end. The reality is that many women have a physical husband at their sides, but they are spiritual widows. For many people, this is the time when one of the biggest battles between most couples begins— the game of who is to blame. Spouses who take the victim roles focus their free time to detail that the reason they are suffering is their partners.

We also find that the vast majority of all marital failures carry someone claiming the role of victim instead of communicating. Why is it so hard for us to just listen to what others say and give them the space to say what they need to get out of their systems. Why is it that without thinking of all the aspects of what they said, we focus on who is right and who is wrong? Why not detail why we agree, or not? We need to understand some people are not open to any options than their own. So what do we do then? Well, then we pray, and ask the Holy Spirit to reveal who is correct. We should also pray that the one who is incorrect assumes responsibility.

The focus and energies that are used in trying to prosecute the guilty occupy greater weight than the shared dialogue in search of a solution. But what happens if the other person does not want that dialogue? Many times it is difficult for people to describe their feelings or emotions. Especially for men. You will find that in their minds, wrong is rarely an option for them, and male pride does not follow too far behind. After all, they assimilate with great satisfaction the head of the household mandate.

I have also heard many men say, "I am the man of the house." This phrase has caused great disputes and arguments. Let's look at both sides of this statement. To be the man of the house, you must first be the man. But to be clear in the role that God gave you, let us first define what it is to be a man according to God's plan. The Greek definition of *anthropo* is root of man. God put man in the garden of Eden, symbolically planting him there to bear fruit.

We know that the fruits usually serve to meet a need, be it food or other. If you look, everything around you is probably the result of something planted. The first mention of man is found in Genesis 1:26, and the first attributes that accompany it are those of recognizing that he also is a creation of God. The next order calls him to bear and multiply fruit. Then, he is ordered to rule over the animal kingdom. At this point, God noticed and declared that "It is not good for man to be alone" (Genesis 2:18). Therefore, when He planted man in Eden, the fruits that God expected of him were the ones to rule, take dominion, and supply Eve's needs.

THE APOSTLE PETER, IN 1 PETER 3:7, EXPLAINS that the woman has fragility. Adam and Eve were called to examine the needs of the other and to supply them. In Eden, God supplied them with everything they could need, but He required that they keep their relationships in order. Detailing it from another perspective, my relationship with God comes first. I have the duty to bear fruit, I must multiply, I must exercise dominion over everything.

The task does not seem complicated. However, we note that in order to complete it, we have to press hard to achieve restraint. Once married, our tasks multiply. The man not only has the duty to supply the financial need of the home but to keep his roles well defined and in place. The steps of Adam went something like this. He was a servant of God first and then a successful man, husband, father, and friend. Everything has its place in life, and our responsibilities are to understand and adapt ourselves to itineraries that allow us to do this without neglecting the other.

It is unfortunate to see that sometimes, something is lost after marriage. Why? The vast majority of us work in secular jobs. As we embark on our workdays, we find that small variations may arise here or there, but we generally do the same things every day. If we are surgeons, the types of surgeries we do can vary, but they will always be surgeries. If we are receptionists, we will answer the phone for different reasons, but we will always answer the phone.

We hear about people who have held the same position for twenty or more years, and we do not stop to think if all that time was without difficult or impossible situations. Let's also ask ourselves if at some point we do not feel a little bored at doing the same things over and over. We also hear from those with the best job offers, but they do not know how to take advantage of them. Good salary and excellent benefits, but they cannot appreciate it. Why not? Because in order to be successful, we have to have a good disposition and a plan for improvement.

No matter what area of life you are trying to develop, you will always benefit from a good disposition and improvement plan! Therefore, if you are bored in your marriage or simply disillusioned; will it not be beneficial to take some time to prepare an improvement plan?

Start with studying your spouse carefully. Rediscover your plans and ambitions. Rediscover their goals and their fears, rediscover their taste and what makes their heart happy. Dare and challenge yourself to fall in love with your spouse's heart again. Rediscover your spouse's body. Put aside any ideals of pride or authority. Focus on the other's great qualities and how well you know your spouse. Wives, see if your spouse still carries the details that made him fall in love with you. If he doesn't, take a quick trip down memory lane, and remember what made him laugh. It's easier than you think.

In the opinions of many spouses, the plan designed by God is only a matter of who has the authority. For others; they only look for the benefits they can obtain from that relationship. They take for granted that the union God created from the beginning was one of love, respect, and mutual help. It has nothing to do with authority. One thinks first about the welfare of his or her spouse.

The meaning of love in detail is found in 1 Corinthians 13:1–13. There Paul speaks of a feeling that even under sacrifice is willing to serve, supply, and cover. It is explained with simplicity that you should be willing to put everything on the line because of the love you feel. In the book of Ephesians, we also find detailed what must dwell in a man who says he feels love for a woman. That is why we should, when entering into a marriage, weigh our feelings rather than our emotions.

This is where we will show our true intentions, and whether pure or impure, self-sincerity is needed. In most cases, unfortunately, we enter into marriage without a clear vision of what moves us. We hear of certain cases where people marry out of necessity. But what usually unites them is a feeling of something that feels like love. But it can also be something else. Understanding this, now let's try to decipher what it is that we feel.

One of the best verses to explain it is found in Jeremiah 17:9, where we find the explanation of the problem. The heart has the ability to deceive us! As human beings, we could avoid many problems if we could productively understand the needs of those around us before thinking about ourselves. The tricky part is to understand that love for another person, before being expressed to him or her, must be confirmed in you. How can I love and care for someone if I don't know what I really feel?

The main thing is to study ourselves first and then the behavior of the other person. That behavior will usually point us in the direction of need. We should not fear or worry as the needs vary. There is an indeterminate number of people who only need to give them a few minutes and listen to them. Others just need to feel supported. But in all cases, only true love equips you with a heart to cover another's need.

Unfortunately those in marriages today know little about their spouses, or only know their bodies. But this will not be enough when we present ourselves before God, who will make us accountable to the love we profess and committed to at the altar. But when we are in love, it will allow us to acknowledge the person and not their faults. "Above all, keep your love for one another at full strength, since love covers a multitude of sins" (1 Peter 4:8).

THE LACK OF DIALOGUE IS A COMMON characteristic of marriages that are struggling. For many spouses, it is easier to talk with outsiders than with the spouse. And we don't realize this disassociation is emerging. This is because for most of us, is easier to accept a difference of opinion from someone other than our partners. And we carry the idea that our partners should accept what we propose. Therefore, there is something in us that makes us think there is an obligation to accept our ideals, whether one agrees or not.

Much friction begins when we fall under the impression that there is something wrong if another doesn't agree with your ideology. But the truth is that on many occasions, what is being considered is not ideal! So then what? Let's use the example of Abraham and Sarah. We notice that Sarah, trying to help God's plan, offers her servant Hagar as a vehicle to receive the son of the promise. It is important to understand that her actions, although perhaps done with the best of intentions, showed distrust of God's promise and poor self-esteem.

As recipients of God's promises, one of the greatest decisions we must make is to understand that promises must always be considered from the point of view of the one who has promised. For example, there are well-interwoven relationships between parents and children. If when we are children our parents earn our trust, as adults, we better understand two subsequent situations. The first is a sense of solid responsibility. The second is a solid relationship with our parents. This arises due to a trust that is born from and based on experience.

But returning to Sarah and her plan B, God promised Abraham the offspring. Abraham had experiences with God, but what degree of confidence had Abraham gained with Sarah? Let's take refuge Genesis 12:10–20. There we find the story of Abraham when he came down to Egypt because of a famine. We notice that for some reason, he recognizes the beauty of his wife but requires that on entering Egypt, she declares to be his sister, not his wife.

Genesis 20:1–18 tells us of another occasion in which Abraham requires her to declare that she is his sister, and God Himself must intercede to avoid sin. Even though Abraham was declaring a half-truth, the intention that led him to decide on that behavior was his own benefit. He was still the bearer of the promise. However, it is necessary to understand that the confidence Sarah could feel in him was a bit deviant.

She saw her husband plotting for his benefit. I think a feeling of disappointment must have arisen in her life. The Bible does not record it, but I believe that even when the customs of that age perceived it as normal, she must have felt uncomfortable with the situation. If we look at it from a different point of view, Sarah received more vindication from Abimelech than from Abraham.

Now, in no way did these circumstances provide Sarah with a justified reason to dishonor or lose the respect she owed her husband. But if it provided a warning voice, it should shake her spirit and put her on alert. It would also be helpful to understand that this alerting voice positioned Sarah to understand she should place every order received from Abraham under the lens of discernment and experiences with God.

The need for direction arises daily. It does not matter what position you are in; if you lean your spirit in search of that direction, you will obtain not only the direction but peace. There is a close relationship between acquiring God's direction and feeling His peace.

Let us now examine this other example; we find it in Exodus 1:15–17. It is explained that the king of Egypt ordered the midwives to kill every male born of Hebrew women. The details pertaining to this order are of a dangerous nature. Because the person giving the order was the king of Egypt, everyone under his reign was supposed to obey. Otherwise, he could execute them. However, these midwives dared to put that order under the lens of discernment. As a result, they decided to obey God rather than men, and the blessing of God did not wait. I mentioned previously the importance of understanding the honor due to everyone. It is in each decision that we show the degree of honor we render.

I would like to reiterate the clarification that we are not trying to project the inability of man to instruct or guide. Just remember that our lives must belong primarily to God in spirit, soul, and body. Then our daily lives should revolve around an initial dependence on the direction of the Holy Spirit in everything we do.

Especially when we occupy the woman's role, we are exposed to ideals that are taught to us from our childhood. In most cases, these carry the potential to deviate from what is truly God's plan for our lives, often ending up serving men more than God. The instructions may vary from person to person, but the only way we can truly develop God's plan for our lives is to stay focused in their direction.

Let's examine this other example, which is found in Joshua 2:1–24. Her story tells us that she lived on the wall of her community. To many, she was known and pointed out as the harlot of the town. Nevertheless, the discernment that she received made her ignore the order of the king of Jericho to expose the spies of the town of Israel. Many would have succumbed to the king's orders immediately. However, her intuition led her to ignore the king's order.

THE PARALYZING FEAR THAT ARISES MANY TIMES due to the demands of those who are supposedly called to guide and direct us could not stop her from letting herself be carried away by what she felt in her heart. The result was that the spies informed Joshua what they saw in that city. And regardless of who she was, she learned that God had mercy on her and her family. God did not wait to bless this action; her family was saved from the invasion that arose in that place.

Let's continue with the story of Queen Vashti. This is found in the book of Esther. Her story teaches us about the banquet that King Ahasuerus and Queen Vashti celebrated. On the seventh day, when the cheerful king of wine ordered that the queen be brought with her crown to show all her beauty, Vashti did not want to attend. This unleashed the king's anger. Her story teaches us that the king's request carried some intentions that she did not see with good eyes. It is necessary to learn that before complying with the demands of those around us. This teaches us that prior to any demand, an examination of the reason for the demand should occur.

We can imagine that her self-respect led her to understand the king's order did not carry a justifiable explanation. Being drunk from the wine, she understood his request could expose her to something that would make her uncomfortable. Many other women, without thinking twice, it would have been the invitation of the century. For her, however, it was a life-changing event.

She was not carried away by emotion or pride. She simply studied the situation and noticed that it did not benefit any area of her life. If we all took the time to examine what we are exposed to, we could avoid many situations that, in the long run, entailed consequences that we would have to live with for the rest of our lives. It does not matter where it comes from. Every situation must be analyzed to determine its inclination.

There is also another very important teaching in this story that we should assimilate. There will always be those who judge what they do not know. Always! There was an immediate meeting to seek the appropriate punishment for the deposed Queen Vashti. It was determined that she would be dismissed. There was no room for dialogue nor time for explanation. She disappears from the story without any complications. This shows us that she was in some way in agreement with the sentence and did not feel the need to fight it. She valued her self-respect more than anything they could bring her way. When we make a decision to do the best we can for ourselves and others, the results will always be inner peace.

Let's continue with our next example. This is in the story of Deborah. She was a prophetess who served as a guide to Israel. It should be noted that the Jews recognized her as a prophetess. Her name means bee, and when the Jews suffered persecution, she served them as a voice of consolation and, at the same time, as a push to attack Sisera under the direction of Barak. However, even when Barak knew that God would give them victory, he refused to go to battle unless Deborah accompanied him. He also agreed with the decision that the victory would be imputed to a woman. This victory inspired Deborah to compose a song, which we find in the book of Judges chapter 5.

We learn from its history a few factors of vital importance. Following the plans he expressed, she would have stayed in fear and not encouraged the men to go to war. She found herself being imparted with insecurity and fear. But she maintained the faith and confidence that the one who was fighting for her people was Jehovah. The imparting of courage and direction that she provided to the people produced the victory that God prepared for them. Another action worthy of admiration was the fact that she did not display any criticism or contempt for the inability of Barak to go to battle.

She seriously clarified what she understood would happen, that everyone would attribute victory to a woman. No reproach, no mockery; simply support and acceptance. One of the most important tasks for a woman is to be able to offer help and support to a man without the need to minimize or belittle him. Always understand that as women, our greatest responsibility is to respect the design that God created and executed, and to let God judge every situation.

We find another great conqueror of the divine plan projected in the life of Hannah. Her story is mentioned in 1st Samuel chapter 1. Her husband, Elkanah, surrounded her with all the affection and care that a woman could desire. Nevertheless, her life was sparce of happiness due to the lack of children. Her rival took the opportunity to sharpen the pain that lived in the heart of this woman. When studying your situation, always note God as the possibility of an absolute solution to your problem. This was to bring her problem before Jehovah and let him be the one to judge its cause. For this woman, as for many others, the resistance was immediate.

Her resistance came directly from the altar of God in the form of a priest named Eli. This not in response from God but because of the little vision of the one who was supposed to minister in the name of the Lord, the priest Eli. As a woman seeking to complete the call that God has made in her life, it is very important to understand that we must be prepared to face resistance in various ways. Hannah teaches us this example of great importance.

It does not matter where the advice comes from. It will only be of value if it is validated by the Word of God. If not, be prepared to succumb. Many of us usually only seek advice when our world feels it is collapsing. The reality is that we have created a society that, in most cases, depends more on external advice than on intuition.

The priest Eli, who was supposed to present Hannah's request, could not discern her true need. He took the attitude of judge instead of mediator. For many people, this would have been a justified reason to surrender and faint. But in Hannah we notice a humble clarification of the reason for her prayer and the decision to understand she left the impossiblity of her situation in the God's hands. We also see the recognition that her life should go on; she ate, she drank, and she was not sad anymore. Many of us spend most of our energy focusing on what is impossible. If we could at least provide God with a glimpse of faith and give Him space to work, then He could provide us with a miracle.

This arises only when we understand that our God is the One who traces the steps of our lives. We might not agree with the setup, but God knows what is best for our lives. He does not need our approval but exposes us to His perfect plan day by day. In diverse situations, He shapes our lives and characters in the vessel that He wants to create. The final recipient is usually one full of blessings and victories that are totally for the glory of God.

Note this step-by-step process through the life of Paul, born as Saul. His story is found in Acts 9:1–9. There we see that through his social position and education, he acquired privileges before the ecclesiastical body of that era. His request was that he be allowed the freedom to bring prisoners, men or women, who were participants in the Christian faith, called those of the Way. He gets a sudden interruption in the form of a visit from a light that makes him fall to the ground as raw material in the creation of man.

He listens from there, on earth, to a voice who interrogates him. Saul was just positioned on the Potter's wheel and could not distinguish it. Gratuitously, God clarified any mistake he made and directed him in the right way. Then we see that once Saul is instructed, he arises from the earth, like a vessel made again. And even when he does not see, he is willing to walk because he understands that all his education and knowledge were null to the absolute sovereignty of God. After that meeting, Saul became Paul and lived a life of service and submission to the King of Kings and Lord of Lords.

It does not matter if you are a man or a woman; we are all exposed to the process of spiritual development. Through that exposure, we can begin to discern the true call that God has made on our lives. We can grow up secularly and reach the top of the world. But from there, you will have to ask what every human being asks at some point: So I was created for what?

Our primary task is and always will be to give glory to God with our lives and ways of life. But we are also called to develop that call He made in our lives. This is the only way to feel whole and happy. There will always be situations that try to divert us from the reason we were created, but our tenacity will keep us focused on complete our calls.

When Jesus declared, "It is finished," He gave us the example to follow. It is impressive to see how many people lose sight of the fact that there is a work to which we are called. We did not appear in the world just to exist; we are called to leave a mark, to make a difference for those after us. We must complete our tasks without ignoring the fact that the glory will be uniquely and exclusively to God.

Returning to the call about women, we also benefit from adding the story of Ruth. Her story teaches us that no matter how great the failure that may arise in our lives, God can create a testimony that gives glory to His name. For those of us who study her life, at first glance, it seems that she would end up being a simple exile from her country. However, God used her situation of failure to place her in one of the most desired positions of that time, what seemed to be an end to poverty and misfortune. God used it to give her honor and wealth.

Our difficult situations and everyday problems are often just the platform that God uses to propel us to deeper levels. That is when we truly begin to know the God we serve. However, it is also this stage where we lose many who, faced with the severity of certain situations, choose to give up and do not fight anymore. It is at this time that we think about divorce. It gives rise to anger and resentment, and we lose sight of the teaching behind all the commotion.

Each case is different in the process, but the end of the process is the same. We must learn to understand that God is in control of our lives—whether we want to understand it or not! So what to do? How are we going to solve this problem? Why can God teach us what He wants to teach us without problems? Why use the difficulty to teach us? Simple, if we notice we are the ones who have the problems with adapting to His instructions. Do you want proof? Adam is created, placed in Eden, and given instructions. And subsequently, we have problems. There are few human beings who like to follow instructions. Everyone prefers to live by their own rules and ideals, and if you want me to tell you, there are no problems with that! But remember in deciding to do so, you will also have to face the consequences.

There are universal laws: if I run, I get tired; if I overeat, I will become fat; if I spend more than what I have, I will need; if I sow, I harvest. Well, then, we should understand that if I am exposed to the Word of God but ignore what I learn there, I will simply have to face the consequences. Now, how do we apply this to the woman's call? After all, we must understand and remember that the head of the household is man. Well, no, that is half true. The head of every home must be God, then our husbands.

When we take the right structure of relationships out of position, we will always confront problems. When we expect more from our spouses than from God, we are in deep water and about to sink. When we expect more of our children than of God, we are in trouble. Having understood all these truths, a question arises. What is the correct position for the woman to assume?

The Bible shows us that God Himself created the first couple, and He provided them with the correct structure to follow. Adam was with God before he received Eve. And Eve was with God before she met Adam. Everything should continue in its established place. It will be then that we will have developed the knowledge to comply with the structure without examining it. After all, who created it? God Himself! Notice that God ordered Adam to fill the earth and rule over it. If you notice, it also tells us that God revisited Adam and Eve and asked, "Adam, where are you?"

Therefore, every plan drawn must be followed by an inspection of achievement. Just as you have raised your children, taught them the difference between right and wrong, and then watched them until they were attached to your teachings. God does it in the same way. He gave them the teachings and then watched to see if they complied with His instructions.

We should continue this same pattern in our positions as wives, mothers, and others. Just as Adam was given instructions, they were also given to Eve. Many of the problems that humanity faces are due to the fact that we are regularly very quick to judge others. We see their faults but choose not to see our own. This does not mean that we should abandon ourselves to the ideals of those who are supposed to be guiding us. We are primary responsible for our relationship with God. Even if that position calls us to follow our spouses, we must understand that if they are not living according to God's call for them, then, as we mentioned before, we are to put every idea under the lamp of the Word of God and act accordingly.

For this reason, we must be very careful not to fall prey to the ideals of those around us. As a woman, we learn from our parents their ideals and customs. When we get married, we are exposed to the ideals of our spouses, who usually are inclined to think that regardless of who we are or how we think, we will follow their ideals. But immediate questions arise: Are these ideals in accordance with the plan that God constituted? Are they aligned with the Word of God?

I think these are the reasons many women have been submerged in life and have not been able to live. I'm sorry to hear the complaints of so many women who, at first glance, seem happy. But at some point, when the cup overflows and happiness leaves, we begin to feel the frustration and disappointment. It should also be said that we cannot judge these women for feeling so discouraged. But we have to accept that fact that this discouragement was due to their commitment to falling in love with a man more than with the care of God. And this will always be a recipe for disaster.

So what to do with this ship that is shipwrecked? What should we do if we have reached a level of disaster? When something does not work, we usually tend to return it to its beginning. This we do to know the reason for the failure. Our lives are not exceptions. When something is not working according to what normal expectation is, it is usually advisable to ask why. Followed by all the questions that may arise, a sincere and clear response should take place. When we ask and conclude the reason, we are placed in the arena of change.

Remember, nothing will be of worth if you cannot be honest in your answers. And if you are disloyal in answering all these questions, you will only be deceiving yourself. Then it would be convenient to raise the pros and cons of each answer. What happens if I do? And what happens if I do not? The next step is to trace who directly or indirectly is involved in the consequences of your decisions. Please take a few minutes, and think what would have happened if you had asked yourself these questions before making your past decisions. You might feel disappointed with someone, or even with yourself. But remember the key is to learn from that error, and refuse to stay stagnant.

I imagine you already have a better picture of where your faults are and how to correct them. Yes, there will be consequences that in some cases you will have to confront. But remember how important it is not to stay stuck. Do you remember Sarah? One of the stages of her life teaches us that at a certain time, we will be confronted with the reality we see versus God's promises. She had no kids, and her body had gotten old. I again want to warn you that regardless of what you see, do no fall into the trap of trying to help God. Of course, the practice of giving her servant to her husband was common in that era, but the help she intended to give God became a sting. However, when Sarah asks Abraham to fire her, who confirms to Abraham that it's okay to do it? Jehovah Himself! Excuse me, but is there something wrong with this picture?

I want to take this moment to ask you to join me in one of the most necessary campaigns to break this circle of failures: this habit of ignoring the importance of educating our daughters. It gives this society a high incidence of women suffering from depression and with low self-esteem. There will be no victorious women, marriages, and families if we do not stop ignoring their education and begin to rescue what has been lost. Let's teach our kids that they are special to God and to us. Adding to that, let's teach them their relationship with God is and always will be the most important one they will ever have.

A common struggle people have is the inability to manage time in order to fulfill our complicated agendas. Many say, "I do not have time." I have even heard myself say, "I need a day of forty-eight hours to do everything I have to do." But the truth is that if we had a day of forty-eight hours or more, we would wrap ourselves even more. Most likely after a while, we would deduce that is not enough time either.

I think that a woman's agenda is often twice as complicated as that of a man. However, many surveys have reported that adaptation to a spiritual and congregational life is much higher in women than men. The results of the last poll I heard reported that for every seven women who attend a congregation, there is one man. I have also heard many preachers say that this is because women tend to be more spiritual or passionate. We do not ignore the reality that there are many men who love and serve God with a passionate and sincere heart.

But it is necessary to clarify with sincerity that God loves both man and woman, and He wants to use them broadly. However, many women will have to force themselves to comply with the ample requirements to which they are called. For this reason, a work plan will most likely provide you with a beneficial tool from which you can obtain broad benefits. Respecting the limited time that we often have to read, I summarize many points looking for the opportunity of a quick but beneficial reading.

To be able to place ourselves in positions of development, let's start with the basics. The apostle Paul, speaking in his first epistle, teaches us in Thessalonians 5:23 that we are possessive beings of a trinity. There he advises us that we must keep ourselves blameless in spirit, soul, and body for His coming.

As a woman in search of conquering the call that God made on your life, it is important that you know everything about yourself. Due to lack of self-interest, we sometimes fall short in developing many areas of our lives. And in many cases, we lack the knowledge of who we are. Personal wholeness is so important and goes hand in hand with feeling complete in soul, spirit, and body. So ask yourself many questions, and see with what you feel identified. Do you feel passion for something specific? Do you have a dream to conquer? Is your spirit balanced?

Remember, if you are spiritually whole but have a sick body, you will encounter problems. The correct feeding, adequate time to rest, and exercise are vitally important aspects to which you owe much attention. All this goes in conjunction with proper medical checkups. You must also understand this should not happen only if you have enough time; you need discipline to maintain this regime.

No matter how busy you may be, you should take time for your personal care. Do not depend on your spouse in areas that you alone can execute; always consult with him without ceasing to execute.

Another area that we should always be diligent in maintaining is our emotional well-being. The fact that you are a woman has placed you on what many have called a hormone roller coaster. It is of vital importance to be alert and well balanced. As we know, our society has been struggling with a stronghold spirit called depression. Without discrimination, it has overtaken men, women, and kids. We have seen that regardless of your race, beliefs, or financial stability, people have succumbed to it. We have the famous, the political, and even clergy dominated by it, so we need to understand the importance of staying focused and alert.

By completing these two areas, you will have placed yourself in the arena of greatest importance to every human being: your spiritual life. As you may have noticed, you entered the world scene independently, alone. This will be the same way that you leave it. This truth teaches us that your relationship with God holds first place. By Him you entered into this world, and only by His command you will leave. Summarizing the basic parameters of our spiritual lives, we know that just as the physical body needs a substantive regime, the spiritual one carries the same need.

We have heard that the food of the spirit is fasting with prayer, and a continuous hunger for knowledge of His Word. We could assume that a spirit not fed with these elements will eventually die. On repeated occasions, I have seen a very common error that, in my opinion, discourages and neutralizes further spiritual development, especially in new converts.

This area is the teaching of intimacy with God. Yes, we are told repeatedly that we must pray and fast. But perhaps we should take the time to teach them to pray and then continuously follow up with them, looking for the experiences they have received from teaching. This visit not only will help us monitor their growth but also give us the opportunity to know if they have grasped the teaching correctly. Few congregations take the time to teach this necessary development area.

Many of today's congregations are full of called Christians who do not know how to pray. The time factor may not always arise. And especially if you are a woman like many others, full of commitments, this may be an uphill task. However, if you truly want to be successful in your spiritual life, you cannot achieve it if you do not pray. God is not impressed by where you do it or by the specific time. He is not impressed by the eloquence of refined words. He just wants to hear your voice. Be audible, silent, or pray in the form of tears and moans. He just wants to hear you.

AS YOU DEVELOP THESE AREAS, YOU WILL NOTICE that your life feels completed. You will feel ready to undertake a search that will be the most important of your life. Something extraordinary arises when you enter this stage of your life. You will notice that although it is important to decide what you are going to study, who you will marry, or the answer to some other weighty decision, nothing can surpass the importance that comes from developing the call of God in your life. Nothing!

You should likewise develop a lot of caution to avoid falling into deviations from your true calling. Remember that the Bible says that the heart is deceptive. It will also benefit you from now on to begin to understand that no matter how far you go, the glory will always be and only be of God. May the call He has made on you be that of preaching, teaching, writing, or any other call that gives glory to God! Find what you are passionate about. Study it, and then begin to develop it in an organized and constant manner after you have confirmed what God has called you to.

Look for those women who before you had the same kind of calling. With respect, learn how they conquered it. But develop a pattern of taking a step and always going back for approval of the One who called you. If you are married and your husband is led by God, he will serve you as a source of constructive critique. Also remember that if he is that man of God, he also has a calling that you should help him with. This is why communication within your marriage is so important. Yes, help him in everything he undertakes. Whether he recognizes your help or not, cover him with your prayers and intercessions. And always prepare the atmosphere of your home so that there is freedom of spirit.

If he has not aligned himself with the calling God has placed on his life, continue praying and interceding for him. But under no circumstances let that stop you. Even if you do not understand what is happening, join him in prayer if he prays, and approach the throne of grace. Always keep in mind that the same God who addresses him is also your God, and He will show you those things that are in accordance with His will and those that are not.

Never underestimate the authority that God has given your husband as head of the household. But be clear on one detail; he is subject to the same spiritual battle that you will have. United, you and your husband will be a more defined team for the battle. Keep him in your active daily prayers. Just as you create an environment for your private time with him, prepare in the same way to unite with your spiritual side. And above all, make sure you stay alert to how your spiritual life is going. Don't be too judgmental with yourself or him. Never forget that God created marriage so that each spouse complements the other.

Let's study what happens when your partner does not execute his main call as head of the household. What position should a woman occupy when maybe she has the physical presence of her husband but not the spiritual one. His body is present there, but he has not come to understand that there is a greater call to which he is bound. Remember, you are studying your husband's behavior to solve the situation, not to criticize but to try to lift.

You cannot achieve anything if you are not first well connected with the Holy Spirit. That is why in previous paragraphs I detailed the need you have to be complete in the Lord. Only an absolute dependence on the Holy Spirit will guarantee you a victory. In the same way, you must understand that the human being is an independent entity, and that service to God is voluntary and of free will. Pray, fast, and intercede for his surrender so that it is God who works in his life. Some will hear the Lord's call, and others may not. But you must respect their free will. He who hears the Lord's call helps Him, restores Him, and thanks the Holy Spirit for His work.

And those who do not hear the call and take lightly the responsibility that God called them to, remember them in your prayers. But never let them harm what God wants to do in your life. You must then assume the responsibility of priestess of your home and enter the spiritual battlefield. Do not let the enemy destroy them! Do not give up, do not stop, and do not be intimidated! I have good news to give you.

This news comes directly from the Bible. Let us carefully study the various stories of women who were confronted with the reality that perhaps the ones who were called to lead them were not executing their call. Through these stories, you will see that the defender of the orphan and the widow physically and spiritually is the Lord. We will see that God was present in all of them.

Eve, when faced with the reality of failure, received a reorganization of her life with new instructions. Even when she had to face the consequences of her sin, God restored her by pointing the right way to go (bear children and fill the earth). Even when God sees our sins, as soon as He perceives repentance, He provides a refocus plan so we can be restored. Yes, we will have to deal with the consequences, as Eve did, but His mercy will always provide a restorative plan.

Continuing with Sarah's life, we find that when Sarah asks Abraham to fire Hagar, God informs Abraham not to think it is serious but to do as Sarah asked. It is impressive how God, who knows the intentions of the heart, works with each one individually. You are not part of the lot; God takes the time to judge your individual situation. To many of us, this is seen as unfair and unjust. However, when God sets a plan for your life, no one—let me repeat, no one—will get Him off His desired plan for you.

And, of course, Hagar is not abandoned either. Our precious Lord also takes care of her. When she is in the desert, in one of the most terrifying scenes a person can experience—the possible death of a child—look who appears, the Lord Himself. This is to assure her that she is not alone and that her son will not die but will have a fruitful life. Hagar's attitude at a given time was not the best, but God corrected and helped her. It seems that when faced with the feeling of failure, we start realizing our mistakes. And because of His great mercy, restoration follows.

Let's continue with the story of Rahab, the harlot. Her name is mentioned in union with her sin. It was like her last name and the reason people felt entitled to point to her as the known harlot of the town. But God is great in mercy and knows the heart of the human being. He does not point her out for her sin, but her story teaches us that she, in union with her family, inhabited the people of God among the Israelites. The men who supposedly loved her could not save her life, but the God who loved her soul provided physical salvation in the moments when all her people died. One of the most loving details of this story is that despite the sin in which this woman lived, she became a vehicle to save the people of God. She was accustomed to serving men. But the Bible teaches us that God always uses whomever He wants, for what He wants, and when He wants. It does not matter what mistakes we made; His purpose is saving us and for our lives to glorify His name.

In all the stories we have mentioned, there is a common denominator. This is the one we must focus on with clarity. We notice that in the failure of man, there appears a God who cares for those spiritual widows and orphans. Even when man is present in the body—many times as guide, teacher, caregiver, and helper/provider—he might be absent. The Holy Spirit is different; you can always count on Him. God never fails. Yes, maybe the solution is not as we expect, but it will always be for our benefit.

Sometimes we feel that although we are accompanied in the physical, in some way, we feel lonely. But I would like to remind you that you are not alone; God is the defender of the orphan and the widow. Even if you do not feel that He is working, He is. If we study the Bible carefully, we find the moments when many women could see how their interventions were present. They could see the glory of God manifested in their favor as you can see it if you can believe.

In Mark 5:25, we see how a sick woman receives the visit of the One who changed her sad condition. The story does not specify if she had a husband, but what we noticed was that she was alone when she decided to approach Jesus, despite the risk that this presented. She had no legal right, no money, no position to approach him. But she made a courageous, determined decision. She focused on the possibility of being healed, not on the condition that labeled her.

Jesus immediately felt the impact of His power, attacking that evil that made her a slave to the contempt and criticism of many. The power that came out of Him healed the body of this woman, and her healing was immediate. Our spirits, souls, and bodies need only a touch of the life-giving power of our precious Jesus. There is a known but recurrent wrong that we have dealt with in most cases. People tend to judge your status with how you appear to be doing. However, there are many times when we find ourselves projecting a happiness that is far from our truths. But always remember that people judge, but God restores.

Let's visit another story that reminds us how precious our Lord's care is. He is the defender of the orphan and the widow. The book of Mark tells us the story of a Syro-Phoenician woman who, having a problem, looks to Jesus for the solution. I want to remind you that at that time, it was not normal for a woman to approach the teachers to ask for anything. Again, we do not know if she had a husband. What we do know is that she was orphaned to the intervention of someone who would help her. So she went to Jesus and presented her need.

Her story teaches us that situations that make us feel lonely may arise in our lives. If a man once offered her his love, he was now gone. Maybe he was physically with her, or maybe he was not. What we do know is that he was not the one who went to seek help in Jesus. That decision left this woman desperate and abandoned of support. This condition also left her daughter, who was tormented by an unclean spirit, without the coverage of a spiritual priest who would intercede before God. There is also the possibility that her husband had died. We do not know, but this did not stop this woman; her need was greater than her instability.

But the most surprising thing about the matter arose when Jesus answered her supplication. It seems that she found Jesus at a bad time. His answer seemed without compassion, abrupt. Even when there was a dislike among the Jews and the Samaritans, it is hard for us to think that our sweet Savior would respond to this woman so coldly. However, this was a lesson for all those present there, and even for all of us who strengthen ourselves by reading His Word. God is no respecter of person, and if we show perseverance, we will get the answer we expect from our Savior. She had experienced man failing her, but not her God.

Let's continue with the story written in Luke 7:11. A woman just lost her only child. She was experiencing the worst kind of loneliness as his company was no longer there. She was accompanied by a large crowd the moment she met Jesus. But it would have been more likely that after the burial and arriving home, little by little, everyone would retire, leaving her submerged in immense solitude.

But her story took an unexpected turn when Jesus found her at the entrance to the city. Our loving Savior was moved to compassion as he saw the pain and anguish that this woman suffered. He ordered the coffin to stop, changing the course of this story forever. We learn from this story that it does not matter how desperate our situation may be. It does not matter how impossible our condition could be. If you notice, this was her only child who died. She was a widow, and he was all who was left of her family.

Many times our tests cause us to lose all hope. We think that there is no way out of our situations. But God reminds us that He is still God and forever will be. The Word teaches us that He is the same yesterday, today, and for eternity. It also teaches that there is nothing impossible for God, and He will be with us to the end. Woman of God, never lose your hope, no matter how hard and impossible your situation might be. Trust in that mighty God, who has never lost a battle, and wait in Him. Remind yourself of His promises, keep your faith, and never lose hope. He is the One who defends the orphan and the widow. So put your heart in His hands.

LUKE 10:38–42 TELLS THE STORY OF A VISIT MADE by Jesus. In this scene, there are two women with very good intentions, but only one made a good decision. This is one of the most complicated areas for Christians to assimilate. In the same way, I have listened to many, including pastors, who have come to the conclusion that there is a great difference between being filled with God and to being full of commitments that involve the call of God. Only self-discipline can help us not to fall prisoners of this dangerous habit. This trick, besides being dangerous, acts as a paralyzing agent, stopping what God has called you to do.

It causes me sadness to hear that even pastors fall into the nets of this custom. As God's people, we have to develop a cunning attitude that alerts us to this devilish ruse. This same attitude is what we noticed in the aforementioned passage. Martha was not acting out of the natural. Their visitors arrived, and it was necessary to assist them. As we noticed, the expected support of one of the sisters took an unexpected turn. So the other took it as natural to go to Jesus and complain about this.

Jesus's response was immediate and clear. He stated that the eagerness of daily life had taken control of Martha, and Mary had placed, "the hand on the good part." We should understand that when the attitude we take is to put the things of God in first place, "it will not be taken from us." No matter how much you think you are covered, how much you are working for the Lord, only surrendering to Him can keep you firmly standing.

If you are a woman full of many tasks, take time to remember that it was Christ Himself who admonished against this. This is one of the best tools used by the enemy to take you out of focus, so you do not execute the plan that God decreed for you. The majority of us become easy victims of this ruse. But God has not abandoned us. One of the most detailed attributes provided through the Bible is His unconditional love for us. If you find yourself buried in eagerness and anxiety, rest in knowing you have at your side He who said, "My peace I leave you, my peace I give you, not as the world gives it I give it." Encourage yourself to promote your peace and the peace of your home. And always screen your to-do list, and make sure your intimate time with God is at the top of your list.

In chapter 21 of St. Luke, we find another story to remind us that we are not alone. Maybe widowhood has come into our lives, or maybe all sustenance has disappeared. However, never forget that He is the defender of the orphan and the widow. We can learn many lessons from this story.

The Widow and Her Kids

I have usually heard most preachers present this story centralized in the ideology of sacrifice, and it is one of the most dominant details of the story. But we also notice the care that the Lord has for those who take refuge in Him.

This widow tells the story by offering all the sustenance she had. She did not give it with regret or waiting to be recognized or repaid. God, who has and orders we are to take special care of orphans and widows, not only recognized it but is moved to mercy. Woman of God, maybe your need can go unnoticed by those around you, but never before God. In your hour of need, do not despair; do not grieve. He is closer than what you perceive.

We find in John chapter 2 the story of the wedding of Canaan and the miracle of Jesus. I love seeing how even when it was not Jesus's time to manifest, as Mary wanted, He did not miss the opportunity to take care of the request that His mother made him. Even when he clarified that what she wanted to happen regarding His ministry must wait, His special care was immediate. He turned the water into wine and supplied the desperate need they had.

In the same way, He knows when you feel your faith has died. If you read the eleventh chapter of John, you will find the story of the death of Lazarus. This death must have been one of the strongest tests for Mary and Martha, his sisters. Remember, he was probably the financial support of that home. Not only did the sadness of losing him develop in them, but they also understood things were going to change for them.

There are times in our lives that can make us feel that everything is over. Situations that have led us to believe everything is lost. This is probably what was in the minds of Martha and Mary. But we must not forget that even when there is no minimum or remote opportunity, if God moves in your situation, life follows; our hopes are restored, and opportunities are renewed. Lazarus was dead, but Jesus is the giver of life. Lazarus's corpse had the stink of death. In Jesus, death can be the moment to glorify and become a pleasant smell to His glory. The hope of a better tomorrow may be the only thing that seems logical, but God is the God of the impossible. He glorifies Himself in our impossible.

Another story that teaches about the way He loves and cares for everyone, specially women, begins in John 20:11, with Mary at the entrance to the tomb where they placed Jesus. Sadness had invaded her soul. She not only cried, but all hope had disappeared. I love the way that the King James Version details the story because it teaches us that while leaning and trying to see inside the tomb, she is surprised by angels who ask her, "Woman why are you crying." Her leaning position describes her situation; she was looking for something to happen. But she hears her name, Mary, in the sweetest form, the voice of the Savior!

Perhaps you feel lonely or sunk in sadness. Maybe you feel disappointed by those who are supposed to be by your side to support, guide, and comfort you. If instead of being recognized for your work, you feel that you are a burden. Or if you feel overwhelmed by all the work you are called to do. Perhaps you feel alone, carrying the burden of raising your children alone. And maybe you feel without spiritual direction from those who were supposed to guide you. Whatever the cause, I want to remind you that Psalm 146 tells us, "The orphan and the widow find support in him."

Maybe by your side there is a physical someone in whom you have placed the hope of a better tomorrow, and now you feel disappointed, depressed, and without a way out. The physical man may disappoint you, but God will always take care of you. He will supply and alleviate your situation. Just trust in God. Remember what it says in Ecclesiastes 5: 8: God is watching over those called to love you, to protect you, to guide you, and to teach you. Maybe they can fail in what He has entrusted them to do, but God will not fail you.

You might ask yourself what to do while abandonment, carelessness, and lack of love are part of your daily life. I can't stress enough the importance of keeping your relationship with God active and constant. In the same way you will have to understand that no matter how lost you feel or feel your family is, trust God. Then you will have to take care of not only keeping yourself submitted to the direction of the Holy Spirit, you will have to be very careful not to be arrested by the spirit of Sapphira.

We find this spirit detailed in Acts 5:11. Sapphira was dragged by a spirit of lies, cover-up, and greed. Her husband knowingly lied to the apostles when it came to revealing the profits obtained in a sale. Peter gave her the opportunity to speak the truth, but she continued to lie, and she finally died as punishment for agreeing to lie to the Holy Spirit.

You know that your relationship with God must occupy the first place in your life. Maintaining this relationship in a healthy state guarantees that you will have the correct direction for your life. You have the opportunity to become the priestess of your home in the spiritual realm. Be careful not to despair and let anxiety and the feeling of failure occupy your mind. You will enter one of the most difficult mental battles you will ever fight. But quiet victory has already been acquired! You only have to go through the process so that you can see it with your own eyes.

You will also have to equip yourself with Bible verses that remind you every moment of God's faithfulness and that He cares for you and your children. And wearing the entire spiritual garment, you enter battle. Do not neglect constant communication with your Redeemer. Every moment keep your guard high, especially in the areas of prayer and fasting.

You will notice that an invasion of contrary thoughts will become part of your daily life. You need to fight them safely through the Word of God. You cannot imagine how much spiritual territory you gain when you do not place yourself in those negative thoughts and concentrate on what God said. You will end the joy of the enemy and give him a massive depression. Make this strategy part of your daily life. Remember all this while you remain alert to the slightest hint of the enemy's attack. You will also need to know the word you are declaring, so get in the Word.

Prepare yourself with at least two verses a day. Read them, repeat them, remind yourself who promised it is faithful. Go ahead; give the enemy a migraine. He hates God's Word because he knows that it carries his downfall. Read the Word, think the Word, and trust the Word. Repeat it again.

ONE OF THE MOST DIFFICULT AREAS TO OVERCOME
is maintaining your trust in God and not in what and
who surround you. It is very easy to succumb to doubt.
Do you remember when Peter stopped, fixed his eyes on
Jesus, and sank in the waters? In our gospel journey, we
are always confronted with this situation. You will not be
the first, nor will you be the last to lose focus on what is
important. Remember also that Jesus did not dismiss Peter
for succumbing to fear and error. He simply reminded him
that our faith must be stable.

There will always be a team that takes the judge's seat and
wants to judge your behavior. Some will use constructive
criticism to show you what is seen from outside the
situation. Others will be severe in giving you the harshest
criticism (not constructive), without worrying about any
damage that may occur. You'll have to take control of
both of them. Avoid giving place to pride when exposed
to a good review, and make sure and control the feeling of
self-sufficiency. On the other hand, do not fall prisoner to

feeling sorry for yourself. Both areas can be very harmful to your growth.

Sapphira was carried away by her husband's ideals. She didn't stop to think that what he proposed was not necessary as no one was demanding they give anything; they just followed what everyone else was doing. The only difference was that their giving was not coming from their hearts. Her mistake was to let her husband's ideals surpass her own. Her customs and values succumbed to those of her husband. We constantly have to remember that we are independent agents, and we will have to give an account to our God at some point.

Remember that salvation is individual. Even if your husband has submitted to God, he can't save you. He can guide you only if he is in sync with what God has called him to do as the head of household. Even when Sapphira's husband was the head of the household, her duty was to examine if her husband's decisions matched those of God. We also note the infinite mercy of God for the human being, since it tells us in verses 8 to 9, where Peter asked her about the sale, as if God wanted to give her a second chance at repentance.

If at that time Sapphira had examined her relationship with God in the personal sphere, she might have felt the Spirit redirecting her. But she seems to have been so focused on the idea of her husband that she gave in completely in union with him. And we see that God's judgment did not wait. In the same place where her husband succumbed, she died. Her actions showed that her submission to her husband was greater than hers to God.

Remember to always keep the nucleus of your home as spiritual as possible. Not only will you benefit, but your children will as well. Perhaps you can become the priestess of your home without losing respect and admiration for your husband. If he is only going through a spiritual low, he may be encouraged to focus on the Lord. You will also have peace, knowing that you tried to help him. Surrounded by prayer, fasting, and intercession, he may be able to rise from where he has fallen.

SURROUND YOURSELF WITH AN ATMOSPHERE OF glory, prayers, and memories of how faithful God has been in His entire journey with you. Read His Word, and let the life in it restore all areas of your life. Let Him take away the pain and the wounds that may be in your heart. Allow His presence to teach you to forgive and not hold a grudge. May the will that He has determined for you shine with its admirable light.

Give yourself the opportunity to live, first for God, then for yourself, and then for yours. Draw a plan looking completely for God's will. And never forget that He who called you was not man but God, and only He has the first place. Develop the discipline of consulting with God before man about all situations. Concentrate on His Word and His will. There is nothing in life that can surpass His love for you. There is no man who can love you how God loves you. There is nothing better than His presence.

Give yourself the opportunity to understand that there is so much you can do to benefit your children and the rest of your family. If you have kids and have examined them in detail, you will probably agree that they, as you, need the spiritual guidance of someone. Only getting closer to God can provide you with the assurance that they will be okay. This comes when you unfold the type of Christians that they might be. We have heard the statement that there are only two types of Christians: those who obey God and those who do not. This is true, but I would like to detail a few facts that might expand those two to three types.

I remind you that when we detail types of Christians, we are referring to Bible-based Christians because the Bible's requirements are always the same. However, when John receives the revelation of the letter to Laodicea in Revelation 3:14–22, there is a warning alert. Since there is a warning, we must study the issue so we can avoid it. Verse 16 details that there are some Christians who will fall into a seesaw syndrome when it comes to serving God.

That will place them in a somewhat shaky relationship; sometimes committed to God and other times indifferent to Him. These lukewarm Christians will eventually have to face their lack of interest in their relationships with God. It also teaches how God feels about that type of relationship. It produces in God some emesis.

So going on, we have the committed, the sometimes committed, and the never committed. Now let's get an example of this. I think we can find an example of these three phases in the life of Peter.

The Widow and Her Kids

As we know, Peter was at one point in the inner circle of Jesus, but he was alerted that he was going to be sifted by Satan. It seemed that he really was not concerned about it. We might say his passion was on the low side at that point. So we see Peter passionate enough that Jesus included him in His inner circle but careless about the warning sign given to him. Then we see him overtaken by the seesaw syndrome when, after all the wonders he saw while with Jesus, Peter returns to fishing after Jesus is crucified.

From one extreme to the other. When we study our and our children's spiritual lives, we should always have in mind that they are exposed as we are to spiritual warfare and will also have struggles. Even if you do not have the help of your spouse in interceding for them, do not dismay! God has you, your kids, and the rest of your family in the palm of His hand.

Remember, Jesus teaches us the need to pray without ceasing. We find this teaching in Luke 18:1–8, where we are presented with a widow who cries out to the king to receive justice because of the oppression of his adversary. But if there is a detail of utmost importance throughout this lesson, it is that Jesus tells us we should ask for the Holy Spirit. Therefore, ask Him in daily prayer that you and your family are supplied with that precious presence. And as the warrior women of God that you are, never forget to intercede for your husband in a very special way.

There is also a call that God made about your life that you must take care of completing. Do not let your past break your future. You still have the opportunity to seize and complete your dreams. God's call has not expired. Do what you once started, and do not be fooled by ideals that are too old or inadequate. If you were called to pastor, shepherd. If you were called to teach, teach. If you were called to sing, sing. If you were called to serve, serve.

IF YOU THINK THAT YOU ARE TOO FALLEN FOR God to save you, I want to share with you this teaching that He thought me when I was down and under. It was a day my cup had runneth over. I remember I was so angry and full of hate that I reminded Him of the worst thoughts and ideas that hit my mind. How unfair life had been from the beginning. I told Him over and over how I hated life and the hypocrisy most people carried and that in reality love did not existed.

I cried so hard that day. I had one task on mind for the day—show God He made a mistake wanting me to leave it all in His hands. After all, if it's true that some of us learn hands on, I had the best possible experience with pain. I could also hurt others the way they hurt me. But He didn't listen. Instead, after I cried all my tears, He said, "Take that doll you see there. I want you to throw it on the floor." I did, and it fell on her face. Then He said, "Pick it up again. And throw it again," which I did. This time, it fell on her back.

Then He told me, "These are the only two ways a person can fall because weight will overtake any other position. If you fall on your head, weight will place you either on your back or front."

I sat there, trying to act smart and make believe I understood. But after a while, I asked, "What does that mean?"

He answered, "If you fall on your face, that is the position of prostration, which implies—whether you recognize it or not—reverence to the One who is above. On the other hand, if you fall on your back, ask yourself what your attention is toward. Whose north? And I, My dear child, can take care of you when you fall and place yourself in a fallen position. Your fallen place is not out of My control. It can't place you in a state from where I can't understand your need of Me." So trust that whatever situation you can be confronted with, you are in His hands.

I MIGHT NOT KNOW WHO YOU ARE OR WHAT YOU are going through. But my sole purpose is to encourage you to examine your current situation and then refocus on becoming whole. You have not placed yourself in a place from where God cannot reach you. I don't care where you are in life. Get up, get up, get up. Refocus and recharge. God has many things in store for you. He is offering His loving hand; pray, seek, and receive. He assures you that He is not mad or upset at you. He reminds you that regardless of your past, He has a great future for you. He will show you that His love will reach you no matter in what condition you are in. He wants to make you whole. He just waits for you to dare, so He can show you His glory.

Epilogue

FAR MORE THAN THE COMPLETION OF WHAT God called me to do is my desire to help those in need. I have learned that God often uses the little things in life to teach us great lessons. And that in most cases, He uses common things to remind us daily He is closer than what we sometimes understand. May this reading serve as a reminder for all those in need that He knows our pain. He knows our hurt, and He is still in control.

Sometimes things will feel unbearable and sometimes out of control. Sometimes we will come to an intersection for which we know of no correct way to turn. Yet He is still in control. Sometimes the little things someone says or something we read, or perhaps something we see serve as reminders that there is a God who watches over us and is in control of everything. Nothing surpasses Him; nothing surprises Him. May we be reminded that our struggles are sometimes the way He draws us closer to Him.